The Mary Rose REVEALED

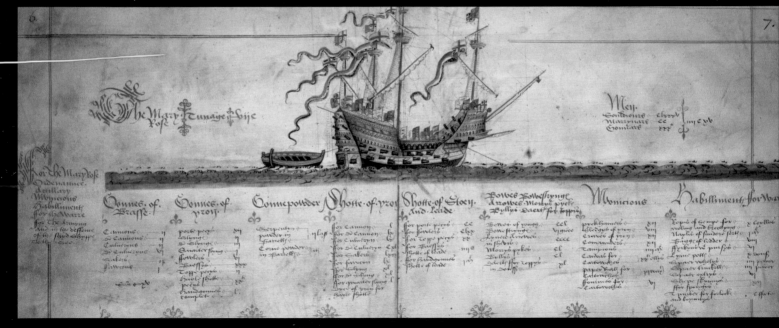

Illustration of the Mary Rose together with a list of her weapons, tonnage and crew. It is one of the 58 vessels illustrated in the Anthony Roll, *an illuminated inventory of all the vessels belonging to the King. Completed in 1546, it is the only contemporary illustration we have Courtesy of the Pepys Library, Magdalene College, Cambridge*

REIGN OF A KING, LIFE OF A SHIP

On Saturday 21st April 1509, aged merely seventeen, Henry ascended the throne of England. His inheritance included an England at peace, an England at the heart of Catholic Europe, a considerable fortune and five ships. His legacy also included a dockyard at Portsmouth, a smaller yard at Woolwich and a Clerk of Ships. Within the year he signed a warrant for the building of two new warships; these would become the *Mary Rose* and the *Peter Pomegranate*. By the time the *Mary Rose* sank 35 years later Henry had a fleet of 58 vessels, an Admiralty with five full-time professional officers and three well-developed dockyards at Portsmouth, Woolwich and Deptford. A new English Church had been formed with Henry as its head and monasteries had been ravaged to pay for Henry's attacks on France and Scotland. He outlived the *Mary Rose* by only two years.

The Young Henry VIII
Anonymous Portrait c 1513
Berger Collection at the Denver Art Museum

Portrait of Henry VIII
Circle of Hans Holbein the Younger, 1497-1543
Art Gallery of Ontario

The Mary Rose: *Henry VIII's Flagship, 1545*
Geoff Hunt PPRSMA

The twenty great warships in Henry VIII's 'Army by Sea'
The Anthony Roll
Courtesy of the Pepys Library, Magdalene College, Cambridge

Great changes happened during the life of the *Mary Rose*, recorded in the hull itself and within the inventories of the weapons she carried. The ship was strengthened, gunports with lids were cut into her sides and deck heights altered to take more heavy guns. What started as a troop ship ended as a gun ship. The weapons industry also flourished to provide weapons for the fleet and for Henry's defensive network of fortifications around the coast. This included Southsea Castle in Portsmouth, central to the scene of the battle which was to end the life of the *Mary Rose*.

TRAGICALLY LOST

Visible symbols of royal power and magnificence, Henry's great warships were both gun platforms and troop transports which supported military campaigns such as Henry's capture of Boulogne in 1544. The *Mary Rose* saw battle in the only two naval engagements of the reign: Brest in 1512 and the Battle of the Solent in 1545, when a French fleet of 225 ships carrying over 30,000 men arrived in the Solent intent on invasion. Henry had assembled his land forces in Portsmouth, encamped on Southsea Common, ready to fight. The French could not penetrate the English shore defences - the channel into the harbour was narrow and protected by the guns of Southsea Castle. So instead they landed troops on the Isle of Wight and burned Bembridge.

The Theatre of The War

Towards evening on the 19th of July the two fleets lay becalmed and at anchor. The English close to Portsmouth, and the French off St Helen's Road anchorage on the Isle of Wight. Four French galleys broke away from the fleet and rowed towards the English ships, firing their forward-facing guns. In the skirmish that followed, the *Mary Rose* sank with 500

Mary Rose *sinking. The last minutes of the* Mary Rose
Geoff Hunt PPRSMA

The English fleet with the Flagship (right) engages the French galleys. The French fleet is shown at anchor (left), with Bembridge on fire (behind)

men, in full view of the King.

The event was so catastrophic that it was recorded several years later in a painting, later copied as an engraving. This records the entire episode in great detail.

The cause of the tragedy is still uncertain. One of the 35 or so survivors records that the *Mary Rose* had fired the guns from one side of the ship and turned to fire again, but dipped her open gunports below the water and sank immediately. Other accounts suggest French gunfire; an unruly crew; a sudden gust of wind; instability; over-manning or over-gunning. Whatever the cause, the loss of the *Mary Rose* ensured her place in history.

Henry VIII on horseback in front of Southsea Castle watches as the Mary Rose *sinks Cowdray engraving, Courtesy Kester Keighley*

Tudor salvage

The loss of the *Mary Rose* was great, both in human and financial terms. Barely a mile offshore, work began immediately to set her upright by pulling on her masts and positioning lifting cables. Removal of sails and rigging was achieved by the 5th August, but attempts to put her upright on the 8th of August failed, breaking the foremast and possibly the main mast. Salvaging of accessible large objects continued for several years. Although a blow to the Tudor navy, their loss was to be our gain.

Victorian intrusion

"We beg leave to report to your Honourable Board that we have discovered by means of our diving apparatus, and picked up in the Anchorage at Spithead a Copper 32 poundr Gun 12 feet long..the Inscription is, HENRICVS VIII". John Deane, 1836.

On the 16th of June 1836, John Deane and William Edwards, diving to salvage the wreck of the *Royal George* at Spithead, were asked to investigate a common fishermen's net snag. It had caught on an old timber, and close by was the gun. At this location it could only have come from one ship – the *Mary Rose* had been found!

Lithograph of John Deane working on the Royal George, *1832. Portsmouth City Museum and Record Services Photograph: Whitstable Museum*

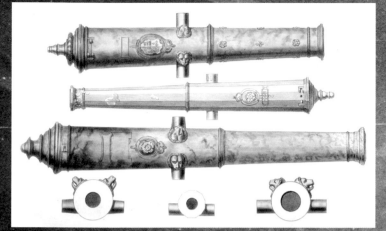

Bronze cannon, demi culverin and demi cannon recovered from the Mary Rose in 1836
Portsmouth City Museum and Record Services
Photograph: John Bevan

Iron grapnel, bottle, concreted shot and longbow recovered from the Mary Rose
Portsmouth City Museums and Record Services
Photograph: Whitstable Museum

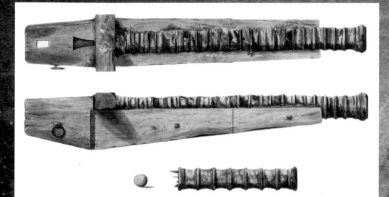

Wrought iron port piece recovered from the Mary Rose in 1836
Portsmouth City Museums and Record Services
Photograph: John Bevan

As only a few objects and timbers were visible on the seabed, Deane and Edwards used spades to dig holes and eventually resorted to using condemned shells as explosive charges to penetrate the silts. Over the next four years, objects including great guns of bronze and wrought iron were recovered together with longbows, shot, a portion of the main mast and a grapnel - many recorded in fine watercolour images. Most were marketed to museums or sold at auction. When the cost of salvaging outweighed the income, they abandoned the project, leaving nearly half a ship protected within the silts.

A pair of spoked wheels and axle are all that remained in 1981 of a port piece in the stern. The gun and carriage had been salvaged by John Deane, over 140 years earlier

REMARKABLY FOUND

The mid 1960s saw the rise of SCUBA diving as a hobby, but for a small group of enthusiasts from the Southsea Branch of the British Sub-Aqua Club, it became an obsession. Led by military historian Alexander McKee, their goal was to search the Solent for historic wrecks, the jewel in the crown being Henry VIII's *Mary Rose*. They called it 'Project Solent Ships'.

Using the scant historical resources available, especially the notes and letters of John Deane, the Cowdray engraving depicting the sinking, and the position of the *Royal George*, areas were defined and searched. A search of hydrographic charts in 1966 yielded a survey of Spithead by Commander Sheringham dated 1841. Four historic wrecks were marked with a cross, including the *Mary Rose*! By 1967, archaeologist Margaret Rule had joined the team and the Mary Rose 1967 Committee was formed to lease an area of seabed around the cross marking the position of the *Mary Rose*, and to secure protection for the wreck when found.

Alexander McKee
Courtesy McKee family archive

1967 Committee dive vessels
Photo: Atlas-Copco

Archaeologist Margaret Rule
learned to dive to inspect
the wreck
Courtesy Nick Rule

The 1967 Committee.
Mrs Margaret Rule,
Cdr Alan Bax,
Mr W O B Major and
Mr Alexander McKee
at the signing of a
Crown Estates lease
of an area of seabed
Mary Rose 1967
Committee archive

Professor Harold Edgerton operating one of his 'pingers' at Spithead, 1968 Courtesy McKee family archive Photo: Alexander McKee

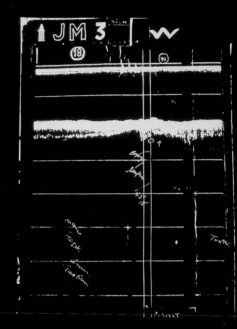

Sub-bottom sonar trace revealing the buried "W" feature Courtesy McKee family archive Photo: Alexander McKee

Structures Revealed By Excavation

metres

Revealed by winter scour
1971

1971

1978

Structure revealed following the 1971 diving season contrasted with the structure exposed by 1978

To find and record ..

Whilst divers scoured the seabed, the search was on for acoustic equipment to penetrate the seabed and reveal buried objects. This came in 1968, with Professor Harold Edgerton and two 'pingers'. Within days a buried "W" shaped feature was revealed. With the search area refined, two years later a wrought iron gun similar to those recovered by John Deane was found. In 1971, following a winter of heavy storms, four timbers in a line were exposed. Later these were indentified as the frames of the port side of the *Mary Rose*.

Self-funded and reliant on donations and sponsorship, work continued following the frames to expose a ship-shape. In 1978 a trench was cut across the bow, revealing two decks *in situ*.

Sleipner, *a converted World War II salvage vessel used in the recovery of the Swedish warship* Vasa, *on tow through the harbour entrance to the site for the first time in 1979*

.. to excavate, raise, bring ashore ..

Following the decision made in 1978 to raise the ship, a charitable trust was needed to raise the enormous funds required not only to raise, but also to conserve and display the ship and her contents. On January 19th, 1979 the Mary Rose Trust was formally inaugurated. His Royal Highness, Prince Charles, the Prince of Wales, who had first dived on the site in 1975, agreed to be President.

Finance was obtained to purchase a diving vessel capable of anchoring over the site from spring to late autumn, and of accommodating a team of divers and diving archaeologists. A programme was established with cut-off points where the site could be backfilled to preserve it if funds were not available to continue. The phases included the removal of silts above the Tudor levels, recovery of all objects inside and immediately around the hull, strengthening the hull, and recovering the ship.

HRH Prince Charles on board Sleipner *discussing progress with archaeologists (l-r) Margaret Rule, Andrew Fielding and Adrian Barak*

*Archaeologist using a paintbrush and
airlift to carefully excavate a personal chest*

PAINSTAKINGLY EXCAVATED

The ship had come to rest on her starboard side in a depth of 14 metres of water. Tides moving across the hull deposited their silts through the open gunports and hatches on the upper port side, rapidly sealing the contents of the ship within a reduced oxygen environment. This silt had preserved over 19,000 objects – each was carefully excavated, surveyed and lifted to the surface. Volunteer divers were given training to use airlifts (which relied on compressed air from the surface) to create suction which removed unwanted spoil down-tide. Excavation revealed objects as fragile as wicker baskets, silk ribbon and plant remains.

Amongst these objects were chests belonging to some of the 500 men who lost their lives. Many contain their possessions and provide intensely personal contact with the crew. Through a study of these objects we have striven to identify their jobs – these collections form key displays within the Mary Rose Museum.

Excavating amongst the remains of chests in the stern, divers support themselves on the grid

A stain in the silt is all that remains of an officer's sword found beside the wooden portion of a navigation compass amongst chests on the upper deck in the stern

OUR SILENT WORLD

Led by archaeologist Margaret Rule, over 500 divers and diving archaeologists undertook over 27,000 dives on the site between 1979 and 1982. A grid was placed over the entire site dividing the work areas into trenches following the main beams of the ship. Substantial portions of three decks survived on the starboard side. The lowermost deck was the storage area for foodstuffs, longbows and arrows, rope lockers and spare rigging. The main deck was the principal gundeck, with six guns found at gunports still on their carriages. The gunport lids were open and the guns run out for action. The upper deck in the stern housed the great cabin, where some of the officers' chests were found, together with the remains of the men who owned them.

Divers worked from dawn to dusk. Following their dives they wrote reports recording the positions of the artefacts they excavated. These 'dive logs' form the basis for placing objects within the large showcases opposite the hull within the museum.

A bronze cannon, still on its carriage on the main deck. Wedged to horizontal for firing, its muzzle still protruded through an open gunport

Archaeological Director Margaret Rule looking for horn tips and bowstrings inside a box full of longbows within the archery store on the lowermost deck

A longbow is raised to the surface

.. to excavate and record ..

As the layers of silt were carefully peeled away, the breadth, amount and condition of the objects became clear. Although primarily a fighting machine, she was also the workplace and living environment for 200 mariners, 185 soldiers, 30 gunners and their officers. As the great timbers of the hull were uncovered, partitions and several intact cabins were found – their occupants and functions suggested by the objects found within. Men, together with their shoes, clothing and some personal possessions were found on all decks of the ship, unable to escape. In the hold and on the orlop deck above, great wooden barrels contained joints of beef ready for a meal. On the main deck a gun in the process of being

An upper deck gunport in the stern viewed from outside the ship

re loaded, on the upper deck handguns lay close to their ports and loose longbows, sheaves of arrows and leather wristguards all confirm that the *Mary Rose* was engaged in fighting in her final moments.

As expanses of the decks were uncovered, objects resting on them were recorded and recovered. The deck planks were tagged, surveyed and photographed by a skilled team of divers selected specifically for this purpose. Excavations outside the ship were undertaken to reveal the hull, and to locate any objects that were preserved around and under the ship. Detailed surveys of the structure were vital for formulating the method of how to lift the ship and how to support it during and after the lift.

A diver swims into view along the main deck
Photo: Patrick Baker

Diver with a long-handled mallet immediately after recovery

A slipped deck plank reveals the supporting half beams below

View towards the stern of the junction of the castle deck and the starboard side. The deck planks have been removed revealing the supporting knees below

Mary Rose EXPOSED

1981 was a tremendous year. Most of the inside of the hull had been exposed and surveyed. What had been discrete trenches were now joined together and it was possible to swim down the length of each of the three decks. Six guns still on their carriages remained in position on the main deck and the cabins of the pilot and surgeon had been excavated. The largest cabin, belonging to the carpenters, was in the process of being excavated. Originally lit by a hanging lantern, work-benches on either side of a central sliding door were covered with tools. Baskets and chests of tools still littered the floor. Chests belonging to the Master Gunner and other officers had slid

Artist's impression of operations. The hull is exposed over a length of 32 metres. A steel grid divides the site into 3 metre wide sections. Divers swim down a rope to the seabed. Three of 12 airlifts on the starboard side are shown releasing unwanted silts down tide
Courtesy Jon Adams

Archaeologist Jon Adams recording the galley structure

Galley bricks

across the deck and come to rest against the outer wall of the cabin. We had perfected lifting these complete with contents to excavate on board 'Sleipner'.

By the time the diving season had ended in December 1981 all the guns had been lifted. It was not uncommon for wire cages containing hundreds of iron shot from the two shot lockers to be recovered for registration and recording before being sent ashore.

Only a few areas such as the brick oven with built-in cauldron remained to be completed, and each brick tagged, recorded and carefully prised from its mortar bed.

Pre-renaissance

In addition to the archaeological processes of excavation and recording was the requirement to recover guns as heavy as three tonnes, and to dismantle as much of the internal structure as possible in preparation for the lift. As decks were exposed and surveyed, deck planks were removed and placed in large containers off site. In total, over 800 internal timbers as well as external fittings such as the rudder and gunport lids were removed prior to the lift. Towards the bow of the ship the main hull timbers became fragmentary and it was necessary to cut the timbers back to solid structure with a chain-saw. Corroded piles of shot and other iron concretions were loosened by using explosive charges or pneumatic tools.

Deck planks and a gunport lid being lifted in an adapted lorry body

Removing a concretion from the castle deck using a pneumatic chipping hammer

Recovery of a bronze demi cannon from the main deck in the stern

Diver tightening a shackle on one of the wire cages full of shot

The method chosen to lift the ship required 170 wires to be securely attached to bolts through the hull of the ship and to a frame positioned over the ship and supported on four legs fitted with hydraulic jacks. Placing the wires required tunnelling beneath the ship to secure the ends of the bolts drilled through the structure from the inside. This tunnelling was achieved by blasting away the sediments under the hull with a water jet to create a pathway for the diver, whilst removing the debris with an airlift. In order to do this work safely, air was supplied to the diver's helmet from the surface via an umbilical. This incorporated a communications link between the diver and the supervisor on the surface.

One of the wrought iron port pieces being winched on board Sleipner

DRAMATICALLY RAISED

Whilst the Mary Rose Trust divers drilled, tunnelled and fitted the lifting wires to the ship, a team of Royal Engineer divers prepared the seabed beside it for a lifting frame and cradle. Made of steel to fit the hull, and lined with air bags, this would support the ship during her final voyage. An 'underwater transfer' of the ship into the cradle required a floating crane capable of lifting the frame suspending the *Mary Rose* and moving it sideways before carefully lowering the ship into the waiting cradle. By early September 1982, *Tog Mor*, owned by Howard Doris, was anchored astern of *Sleipner*, dwarfing her and dominating the Solent seascape.

Inch by inch, the hydraulic jacks on the legs of the frame performed their task, gently prizing the *Mary Rose* out of the seabed.

At 9.03 on October 11th 1982 the *Mary Rose* surfaced to the sounds of klaxons blasting from the myriad of small vessels gathered to watch. From Southsea Castle, where Henry had witnessed the sinking of his great ship 437 years previously, a gun salute could be heard. Around the world 60 million people watched the longest

The Solent in October 1982. Sleipner, Tog Mor *and Spitbank Fort*

television outside broadcast yet undertaken, as *Mary Rose*, sandwiched between the lifting frame and cradle, was carefully lowered on to a barge for the short tow home to Portsmouth.

The Mary Rose *suspended by* Tog Mor. *The Prince of Wales's Standard shows that His Royal Highness is on board* Sleipner

Mary Rose salvage team divers Paul Chisholm and Simon Jones inside the hull immediately after the lift

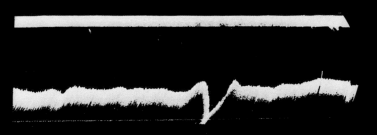

Sub-bottom profiler section through the seabed showing the hole in the seabed left by the raising of the hull

The Mary Rose salvage team with Margaret Rule, HRH Prince Charles, King Constantine of Greece and Lord Romsey

HOMECOMING

In air, away from the water and silt that had protected her for so long, *Mary Rose* was at risk. Without immediate care her timbers could rapidly dry out, shrink and crack. Before she left the wreck site the pumps attached to the lifting frame above her began their work, constantly spraying her with water. Her home was to be, and still is, Number 3 Dry Dock in Portsmouth Harbour. Itself a listed historic monument, it is within metres of where she had been built 472 years before, and beside Nelson's flagship, HMS *Victory*.

Now it was crucial to provide a secure and sheltered building over the ship where the process of conserving the ship could begin. Between February and October 1983 a huge building made of aluminium arches covered in an insulated double skin of man-made fibre was built over the ship, with a viewing bridge constructed over the bow. On October 11th 1983, exactly a year after she was raised to the surface, *Mary Rose* was open to visitors.

To wash out the salts, the hull was sprayed with chilled fresh water for all but several hours a day. During these precious minutes archaeologists expanded surveys of the hull started underwater.

The Mary Rose, *still supported on her cradle, entering No 3 Dry Dock*

The position and condition of every iron bolt and wooden treenail were plotted. Areas inaccessible whilst the ship was underwater were explored and recorded in fine detail. A survey of wood samples was taken of the timbers to assess their condition and used to plan the detailed conservation programme. Many of the 800 timbers removed from the wreck underwater were reinstated, and the hull began to look like the ship we remembered as the deck planks were replaced, deck-by-deck, all in public view.

Fourteen metres above the floor of the dock, the roof of the Ship Hall takes shape

The Mary Rose within the mist. She remained on her side, as she was on the seabed, until the cradle was turned upright in 1985

MIRACULOUSLY PRESERVED

This period of spraying with chilled water stopped the timbers from drying out and inhibited fungal and bacterial growth. It continued for twelve years, all of this time accessible to the public. Although the timbers retained their shape, much of their internal cellular structure had degraded. These needed to be strengthened before the hull could be dried to avoid collapse. The chemical chosen for this was polyethylene glycol in solution, sprayed over the ship for a period of years, increasing the molecular weight of the chemical and increasing the temperature as the timbers absorbed it. During this period the viewing galleries had to be glazed, and the conservators and archaeologists had to wear protective clothing. The warmer temperatures were an ideal environment for bacteria and fungi.

As the new museum was built over and around the ship, she was protected, shrouded within an insulated box. For the first time the ship was excluded from public view until the building was completed. The final stage in the conservation treatment is drying

Wearing a protective suit and breathing apparatus, Conservation Manager Glenn McConnachie inspects main deck timbers at the stern. These inspections were carried out throughout the time the hull was sprayed with PEG. Built-in radio communications enabled the conservator to address the public through a PA system in the viewing gallery

View of the inside of the starboard side looking from bow to stern at the level of the upper gundeck. All of the wooden structure is original timber; any supports required were manufactured in titanium

the ship with air, supplied by fabric ducts suspended throughout the ship. Currently there are a number of large viewing windows on three levels to enable glimpses of the inside of the ship. Once dry, the hull will be displayed in an open museum environment once again.

Access to maintain the spray system and sample the timbers requires a crane with personnel bucket. The ends of the huge beams supporting the main deck show evidence of holes left by marine borers as the port side of the ship deteriorated to seabed level

View of the outside of the sterncastle on the starboard side looking towards the bow. The small holes are ports for handguns. The rail and chain-plate running the length of the sterncastle are to provide hold-fasts and spreading points for the rigging and chains tensioning the shrouds that support the masts. The outside planking of the ship from upper deck level is made of overlapping clinker planking. A gunport for a bronze culverin can be seen in the distance

The outside of the starboard side of the ship. View towards the bow and down on to the upper gundeck from castle deck level. This is the open 'weather' deck between the two castles. Netting would have been strung over this area with a series of removable blinds between the vertical standards. Note the main deck gunports (right)

SAILING THE SHIP

Although much of the rigging was recovered by Tudor salvaging, elements from the standing rigging were found beneath the starboard side, some still attached to the ship. Cable from one of the two rope lockers lay draped on the upper deck amidships, beside an iron anchor. On the storage deck we uncovered a rigging store, with blocks, a spare set of parrels – trucks (balls) and ribs used to 'roll' the sail carrying yards up the masts, and a complete crow's nest or ship's top. The vast array in style of rigging blocks, many with bronze sheaves, indicate that a multitude of sources was required to meet the huge number of blocks needed.

This was an age of exploration. Eleven years after the *Mary Rose* first sailed, Magellan circumnavigated the world. But the *Mary Rose* did not. Her role was to patrol the 'Narrow Seas', dividing England and France, and the North Sea to Scotland. During his reign Henry waged war on both countries, occasionally simultaneously. But navigation and pilotage was crucial, many hazards lay close to shore. In 1514 Henry established Trinity House to train mariners and maintain buoys and lights. Our instruments represent the toolkit of the coastal navigator and pilot; compass, tide calculator, sounding lead, log reel, and sandglass. No charts survived, but chartsticks, dividers and a protractor did. It is the earliest dated set of navigational tools in Europe.

Parrel trucks and rib, rigging blocks and cable

Wooden cover and base for a compass, chartsticks and dividers with their case

One of three compasses recovered. Held on brass gimbals, this moved with the ship to keep the needle level

A selection of lead weights. The larger ones have a dimple in the base which would be filled with tallow wax and lowered to the seabed, sticking to the sediment. This provided details of the water depth and seabed type

A wooden log reel. This would have a rope wound around it attached to a wooden float. Timed by a sandglass, this float was trailed behind the ship and used to calculate speed

ARMED FOR WAR

The *Mary Rose* was built for war. At her launch she carried 78 guns, when she sank, 91, excluding hand-held guns. Thirty-nine of these were large guns on carriages stationed at ports cut in the side of her hull. The only contemporary illustration, the unique painted and gilded image of her above the inventory of her weapons drawn by Anthony Anthony, shows her bristling with guns. The size and breadth of Henry's fleet was a statement of power, the actual power was embodied within the great bronze guns, embellished with royal devices, many bearing the initials 'H I' – Henricus Invictissimus', (Henry most invincible). Warfare at sea had changed during the life of the ship – fighting **with** the ship replacing

Muzzle of one of the long-range cast bronze guns. Fifteen of these were carried, distributed over four decks

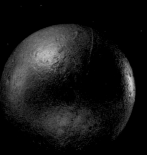

Cast iron shot. Many bear the mark 'H' for Henry, cast within the shot. Over 1200 were found

Selection of round shot made of stone, cast iron, composites of iron and lead, and cast lead. Over 2000 were recovered

Loading implements. Powder ladle, top of a powder horn, linstock for igniting the gunpowder, shot, wooden tampions used to seal powder chambers, brass reamer to clean out the touchhole and pierce the gunpowder cartridge

Small gun cast in iron. Supported on a rail and held under the arm, these are the first evidence for casting large numbers of guns in iron. Iron was locally available and much cheaper than the foreign copper needed for bronze guns. With their rectangular bores, they fired small dice shot of iron, which scattered and injured anyone in their path

The basket-shaped hilt of an officer's sword, and the only complete sword found. The finding of this sword, precisely dated, confirms an English origin for this type of hilt

Ends of yew longbows within their poplar box. 179 of the 250 longbows listed in the Antony Roll were found. The archery assemblage recovered is the most important in the world

fighting **from** the ship, and engaging at ever increasing distances.

She carried a mixture of guns of different types and sizes, for specific purposes and firing particular types of shot. On the main deck the most powerful modern long-range cast bronze guns sat beside wrought iron guns with removable powder chambers. The former the more powerful, and the latter, swiftly re-loaded with stone shot, created great gashes in ships' sides at closer range.

Henry encouraged a domestic weapons industry, supporting foundries in London and Sussex. The first attempts to mass-produce cast guns in iron are demonstrated by the hailshot pieces recovered. Handheld weapons included musket-like handguns imported from northern Italy, the traditional yew longbow, anti-boarding weapons such as bills and pikes, and for intimate action, the sword.

Royal ornamentation on one of the bronze guns. Henry VIII's coat of arms, his monogram and the Tudor Rose badge

Main deck viewing gallery with the guns placed as they were within the ship. Viewed from the bow towards the stern

Tending the ship – The Carpenters

The ship's carpenters were the engineers of the sixteenth century. In a world of wood, they were vital, and worthy of the large cabin they shared on the main deck towards the stern. Within the cabin and around the ship we found evidence of their labours – over 200 tools in all were found – mallets, augers, planes, rulers, adzes, axes, hammers, handsaws, spokeshaves, gimlets, braces, chisels, and whetstones. The scope of tools and personal possessions from chests inside the cabin suggest that up to six carpenters may have been on board. On the deck just below the cabin a single individual was found with his tools – a sawhorse, hammer, chisel, chopping block and tool holder were found. Was he working here when the ship capsized?

The chest belonging to the Master Carpenter contained some of the most expensive and beautiful possessions recovered, and his story is told within a special display in the museum.

The carved underside of a poplar whetstone holder. Twenty-one whetstones were found for sharpening tools, 11 either inside or just outside the cabin

Some of the 22 woodworking planes found. Most were found in chests just outside the cabin

The inside of the carpenter's cabin with contents. Reconstruction based on dive logs

Selection of tools for maintaining the ship

Objects found within the Surgeon's cabin. Stoneware medicine jars, shaving bowl, pewter canisters and pre-made bandages, bleeding bowl, copper bowl and chafing dish, pewter bottle and plates, wooden spatulas, urethral syringe and wooden canister

TENDING THE MEN – THE SURGEON

In the closely packed community on board the potential for the spread of infection was great. Everyday handling of the ship brought its dangers, as evidenced by the thirty or more healed fractures observed within the crew. On a ship at war the chances of injury were high. Within a cramped, unlit cabin on the main deck the Surgeon kept his tools. Although surgery was probably limited to bleeding, amputating wounded limbs and cauterising these to promote healing, he also acted as apothecary, physician and dentist to the 500 men on board. The cabin contained a bench for preparing dressings – bandages soaked in herbal preparations – and a wooden chest which contained 64 objects. These included wooden lidded canisters containing ointments, corked stoneware jars made in Germany, probably imported with their liquid contents and rolls of pre-prepared dressings for immediate use. Urethral syringes for the treatment of venereal diseases were found within the chest as well as a trepan for drilling into the skull and the handles of a number of other surgical tools.

Detail of pewter canisters and syringe, stoneware jar and two-handled jug from Portugal. Analysis of the contents revealed fern oil that had been mixed with milk

The Surgeon was a highly paid member of the crew, and although we do not know his name, his cabin, surgical chest and personal belongings reflect his importance, and his story is told within the museum.

Stoneware jugs from Raeren in the Netherlands, near modern day Aachen

Small tin-glazed jug made in the southern Netherlands. It is finely decorated. Its size and decoration suggest that it contained a precious liquid needed in only small quantities

THE LIVING SHIP

At sea, as on land, there was a huge social gulf between the officers and the men. The officers ate off elegant pewter tableware; they wore fashionable clothes trimmed with silk, the finest leather boots and the newest style in shoes. They had personal possessions neatly folded within sea chests containing purses with coins and dice for gambling. They had books, their own decorated pewter drinking flagons, wicker-bound wine flasks, pepper to add to their food and even some jewellery. By contrast, many of the men went barefoot on board, ate off wooden dishes, drank from their own wooden bowls, and wore simple clothing of leather, wool and linen. It is these simple objects of wood and leather, the mundane objects not worthy of passing from generation to generation, that form the majority of the collection. The sinking of the *Mary Rose* has provided us with a unique insight into everyday domestic objects, like looking into a Bruegel painting.

Carved bone plaque depicting two angels carrying candles. This is one segment of a casket made of similar plaques. It is from northern Italy, and common in the 15th century. Was its owner a foreigner?

This boarded oak stool is one of the few items of furniture which survived. Pewter objects include serving platters, dishes, serving flagons, spoons and flasks. Many have the marks of their makers and some have the initials of their owners

Simple turned wooden bowls and dishes, decorated leather flagon and the boxwood handles from the ubiquitous ballock knife. Many of the bowls have crude initials or geometric designs carved into them to denote ownership

Boxwood comb and leather pouch. Over eighty combs were recovered, the fine teeth are for lice and nits, and the larger teeth are for grooming

Some of the 29 gold coins recovered. The majority were called 'angels' and had a ship on one side and the winged figure of St Michael on the other. These were worth 8 shillings – 40p. The larger coin is a ryal. Worth 50p, this was made in Coventry 80 years before the ship sank. The smaller coin is a half angel

MESSING THE MEN

'Cawdrons in furnos with their apparell'

Deep in the hold lay the 'kychen'. Two huge brass cauldrons, each holding up to 400 litres of liquid, were set within a brick structure which included two wood-fuelled ovens accessed by arched entrances beneath the cauldrons. Made of over 2,000 bricks and straddling the keelson, the central internal backbone of the ship, this was the galley.

With bread baked in the ovens, meat dangled over the oven entrances to roast, pottery vessels filled with separate meals for the officers, and muslin sacks filled with peas or greens floated within the cauldrons of simmering broth, this was the Aga of its day. It was also the domain of one of the most important men on board, the Cook. Paid as much as the Master Carpenter and Master Gunner, the Cook and his galley are special features within the museum. One bowl was carved with the words "NYE COEP COOK", was this the name of our Cook?

Experimental archaeology. A joint roasts over the oven entrance

A muslin sack containing peas is cooked within the broth

Secrets from the silts

Evidence of the food on board was found within some of the thousands of silt samples taken during the excavation. Some were obvious: the remains of half pig carcasses found near the galley, the eight barrels filled with portions of butchered cattle, baskets full of cod or hake, conger eels, and a basket with plum stones. The careful sieving of all samples meant that even the smallest remains such as the residue of grapes from a seemingly empty barrel could be identified.

One of the hundreds of oak barrels during excavation. Each stave was numbered and tagged before being taken apart so that the barrels could be reconstructed. Contents were carefully placed into modern containers for analysis

Environmental archaeologist Ian Oxley sieving the contents of a container. These were passed through a series of sieves of decreasing sizes and the contents separated. The residue left was kept for more detailed analysis

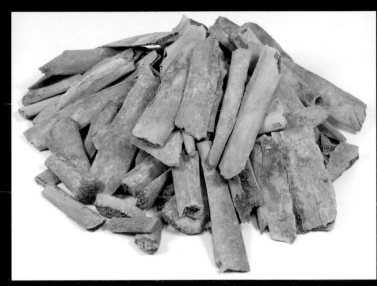

Some of the 1,000 cattle bones recovered, butchered into standard portions

Pig ribs from the deposits of carcasses found on the storage deck near the galley

PRESERVED FOR ALL TIME

Once uncovered from their protective mantle of silt, nearly all of the objects required treatment. The method adopted depended on the material, the degree of degradation, and an understanding of the process of degradation. Most materials required desalination, sometimes taking years, to remove the salts. Organic materials such as wood and leather required impregnation with a bulking agent to reinforce some of the degraded cells. Solutions used included chemical waxes such as polyethylene glycol, or mannitol (a sugar alcohol). Most objects were then put in freeze-drying chambers to remove the water under vacuum. Some objects, such as the ship, are being dried slowly in air. All will then require surface finishing and display or storage within controlled environments.

Conservator Sue Bickerton applying the final surface treatment to the only sixteenth century mast top in the world
Photo: Peter Langdown

The largest single object to undergo conservation is the hull. The final stage is air-drying, estimated to finish in about 2017

Gun carriages being removed from one of the freeze-dryers. The water has been removed under vacuum, leaving the wax within the wood to provide support

Metal objects were treated in a number of ways depending on the material and its condition, so many treatments were bespoke. These included stabilisation using reduction techniques such as heating in an atmosphere of hydrogen, or reduction by electrolysis. Others were treated by long-term washing in deionised water and then coating with corrosion inhibitors. Some of the pewter and bronze objects were intensively washed, then dried using solvents. Most metal objects were coated with a wax or acrylic lacquer to protect the surface.

Larger objects, such as gun carriage parts, were placed in large tanks for soaking in polyethylene glycol

All the showcases within the museum have controlled conditions of temperature and humidity

King's ship – Prince's passion

His Royal Highness, Prince Charles, The Prince of Wales, on board Sleipner *during the raising of the* Mary Rose *in October 1982*

"The result of all this hard work and expertise is that future generations, we hope, will be able to glimpse a small part of Britain's maritime heritage; will be able to see history "come alive" and to step, as it were, into the shoes of a Tudor seaman in the reign of Henry VIII. The only real way of understanding and coping with the present is, I believe, through an adequate knowledge and interpretation of the past. From that point of view we are able, for once, to transform a contemporary naval disaster into a victory in terms of human awareness".

HRH Prince Charles, Prince of Wales, 1982

Prince Charles, President of the Mary Rose Trust, has maintained an enthusiastic and active interest in the project since his first dive in 1975, even before the Trust was formed. His ninth (and to date his most recent) dive was undertaken in 1982, immediately before the raising. He was one of the first people to get close to the hull after she was raised, and has maintained close ties with the project throughout.

He spoke of diving conditions as *"like diving in cold lentil soup"* and of the experience, he said: *"For me it was a great thrill. A feeling of connection with Henry VIII made it even more intriguing".*

Kitted up and being briefed before a dive in 1980

Looking at one of the pewter jars from the Surgeon's chest in 1980, together with Archaeological Director Margaret Rule and Finds Supervisor Andrew Elkerton

On the main deck in 1981. Examining the spoked wheels from a carriage for an iron gun in the stern

Preparing for an inspection dive on the wreck immediately before the lift, 1982

Reminiscing with members of the Mary Rose Salvage Diving Team, October 11, 1982

With Lord Caldecot, Chairman of the Mary Rose Trust and Richard Harrison, Chief Executive, at the opening of the first Mary Rose Exhibition in 1984

As Founder Member of the Flag Officer's Club, presenting Mr Peter Mallinson with his Vice Admiral's sword

Our 21st century diving support vessel, Terschelling, moored over the site

21ST CENTURY EXCAVATION

The raising of the hull in 1982 left a large hole in the seabed exposing the Tudor seabed beneath the ship. Any erosion to the sides of the hole could endanger objects buried around the site, and so a programme of regular site monitoring was initiated in 1983. But in 2002 a new threat loomed, one posed by the Ministry of Defence. A deeper and wider channel into Portsmouth Harbour was required for two new aircraft carriers – and the best route was straight through the site. The site of the *Mary Rose*, one of the most advanced and well-armed ships of her time, was being threatened by her 21st century counterpart. Part of the evaluation included re-assessing the potential threat to the Mary Rose site, and in 2003 the MoD provided the funding for us to undertake this study.

The crawling excavator. This was positioned offsite and guided to the spoil mounds before deploying the airlift. Two cameras enabled the pilot to see both the work face and the orientation of the vehicle

Divers entered the water using a wet bell that provided an elevator to and from the site. All diving was using surface supplied air through umbilicals

Diver with 'Mr Sticky', an acoustic transducer mounted on a pole. Positioned over objects, acoustic signals from four transponders on the seabed position it accurately

Archaeologist recording the stem timber

Remote sensing provided a plan of magnetic hotspots, buried 'anomalies' and surface features – all were investigated. We used a remotely operated crawling vehicle fitted with cameras, location devices and an airlift attached to a sieve to dig trenches into the spoil heaps which had built up on either side of the hull between 1979 and 1982. We recovered over 400 objects and found the end of the ship's stem, the huge timber that rises up from the keel and defines the shape of the bow. Funding continued for the next two years and excavation revealed a portion of the missing port side of the ship in the bow. On October 11th 2005, 23 years to the day since the ship was lifted, the stem was recovered, along with a huge bow anchor. And the missing part of the port side – reburied for future generations.

Site plan of the large structures and objects found between 2003 and 2005, and their location relative to the original hull of the ship. The blue shadow is the original projected shape of the aftercastle and forecastle, the red shape is the slightly new orientation of the bow after the stem broke away from the ship Site Recorder Plan. Peter Holt

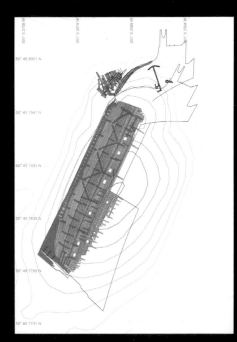

October 11, 2005, the stem of the Mary Rose is raised

REALISING DREAMS

Even before the ship was found, the Mary Rose 1967 Committee was formed to protect it **when** it was found. Amongst the objectives were "To display for all time in Portsmouth the *Mary Rose*" and "To establish, equip and maintain a museum or museums in Portsmouth to house the *Mary Rose* and related or associated material". This persevering optimism underpins every aspect of the project and undoubtedly contributes to its continuing success. The Mary Rose Trust adopted those objectives, and bit-by-bit has fulfilled them. The ship was raised, opened to the public a year later and a museum housing the associated artefacts the following year. But the dream was always to house the ship and her collection together, within one building, as found, as it should be.

The new Mary Rose Museum stands beside HMS Victory *and close to where the* Mary Rose *was built in 1510*

The concept. Walkways at three levels are designed to enable viewing of the ship to one side, with long galleries on the other
Courtesy Pringle Brandon Perkins + Will

In 2005 it was decided to build a new museum over and around the ship whilst her conservation continued. This was a considerable challenge – the space available had a number of constraints and the dry dock housing the *Mary Rose* is itself a Grade 1 Scheduled Ancient Monument. The architects chosen were Wilkinson Eyre and Pringle Brandon. The concept of the building is based on an oyster shell, with the *Mary Rose* the pearl at its centre. The museum is on three levels; with long galleries running the length of the ship to represent the lower decks, main deck and upper deck. Walkways between the galleries and the ship afford views in one direction into the starboard side of the ship, and in the other direction into the galleries where the hundreds of objects are positioned as they were found. Until the conservation is complete, the ship will be viewed through viewing ports, but by 2017 the dividing wall should come down and the ship will be on open display beside the walkways.

At both ends of the walkways are further galleries that explore and interpret the collection. The personal and professional belongings of specific crew members have been selected to present their stories and to provide unrivalled insights into the lives of officers and men both at work and also at leisure.

View down the main deck walkway. Windows on one side of the walkway access views of the ship, whilst the objects found within that space on the ship are repositioned within the glazed gallery, opposite where they were found
Courtesy Pringle Brandon Perkins + Will

View of main and upper deck gallery Courtesy Hutton+Crow

THE ULTIMATE SACRIFICE

The men of the *Mary Rose*

An engraved slab of Welsh slate marks the resting place of an unknown member of the ship's company. On July 19th, 1984, an anniversary of the sinking, a Requiem was held in Portsmouth Anglican Cathedral to remember and give thanks for the lives of the 500 who perished over four centuries earlier. Through a miracle of preservation, their deaths have left a rich legacy for generations into the distant future.

WHEN THEIR WORLD ENDED, OUR STORY BEGAN

Intimately associated with the thousands of artefacts were the remains of the crew, only 35 of whom are thought to have survived. Human remains were found on all decks, the swiftness with which the *Mary Rose* sank did not allow time for escape.

The remains of 179 individuals are represented, 92 have been partially reconstructed. All were male, most in their 20s when they died, the youngest around 10 and the oldest over 40. The average

An unknown member of the ship's crew is laid to rest

height was 1.71 metres – slightly smaller than UK males today. Some suffered childhood illnesses, mainly malnourishment, and there are healed fractures and some battle injuries, but in general they were healthy. Some bones have provided clues about the life of the individual. Reactions to the stresses from routine use of heavy warbows, or handling large guns, are visible on some bones, enabling us to suggest a profession for some individuals.

The skeleton of an archer found on the main deck. Beside him, his bag full of arrows

Carpenter

Master Gunner

Officer

Gentleman

Archer Royal

The Purser

Some of the 400 shoes belonging to the crew

The Cook

Archer

'Hatch'

The Archer from the Hold

Key crew members have also been identified by where they were found – such as the Cook found in his galley – or by the objects found with them – the Master Gunner, three of the Archers, the Purser, Officer and Gentleman. The Surgeon is represented by his cabin, chest and the objects therein. Personal possessions give us some idea as to the nature of the man. These 'characters' have been given their own cases, where their objects are displayed and their lives explored.

To help visualise individuals, facial reconstructions have been undertaken based on a study of their skulls. Using techniques more often used in forensic reconstructions of crime victims, we have re-created the faces of nine individuals. The most complete skeleton, an archer found in the hold, is displayed in full, beside a life-sized model. Similar scientific approaches have been used to identify the breed, colour and hair type of 'Hatch', a small dog found in the doorway of the carpenter's cabin.

LEGACY

The sinking of the *Mary Rose* was by all accounts swift; she did not blow up, she did not catch fire. She sank on her side into soft Eocene clays that allowed her to settle into the seabed. The morphology and position of the Solent give rise to unique currents; these caused the rapid deposition of fine sediments, producing the anoxic conditions which preserved the ship and her artefacts.

The Mary Rose Trust, and before it the Mary Rose 1967 Committee, were responsible for finding and investigating this buried wreck, and so began to alter the environment which had preserved her for so long. The rich legacy that has come from the excavation and raising have therefore come with a commitment. This was understood and enshrined within the aims and objectives of the Mary Rose 1967 Committee and later the Trust. "To find, record, excavate, bring ashore, publish, report on and display **for all time** in Portsmouth the *Mary Rose*". We have been successful in reaching all of these objectives, but we have an ongoing responsibility to maintain them.

Part of this legacy has been the acquisition of skills and the invention of techniques required to excavate, conserve and display the collection. We are sharing these through internships within the Trust, and through our staff advising on or leading other projects, serving on committees which determine the future of these disciplines, and teaching at all levels.

The site

We still have an ongoing commitment to the protection of the site where the *Mary Rose* lay. The Mary Rose Trust holds a lease to the seabed in which any unexcavated remains of the vessel lie. Under the 1973 Protection of Wrecks Act, which designates an exclusion area around the site, we hold the licence to dive. The 2003-2005 diving programme uncovered a section of the port side in the bow. This was surveyed and reburied under silt, a membrane, two layers of sandbags and 80 tons of loose sand. We still have many unanswered questions and know that portions of the forecastle still remain to be found. At present we will continue to monitor the site, assured that there is still more of the Mary Rose legacy for archaeologists to explore in the future.

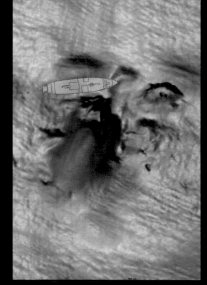

The buoy marking the position of the site of the Mary Rose

Survey showing the seabed in 2005. The rectangular area between the ship and the hole is where the port timbers

Some of the 80 tons of sand used to rebury the port side timbers